A Viking's Guide to Wealth and Health

Simple steps to help YOU become wealthier and healthier.

John Bredvik

A Viking's Guide to Wealth and Health
Simple Steps to Help You Become Wealthier and Healthier
By John Bredvik

First Paperback Printing, August 2021
ISBN 978-1-7376945-0-2

Printed in the United States of America

DEDICATION

This book is dedicated to all of you who know there is more to life and to those of you who want and desire to be wealthier and healthier. I dedicate this book to all of you who have believed in me and have shown me that you can indeed fly by flapping your arms!

Dec 2021

Annie,

You are a great pal!
I love our friendship &
Enjoy the book.

JB

CONTENTS

ACKNOWLEDGMENTS

Many thanks to my pal Jeremy Davidson. Without Jeremy, this book would not be the active, living, breathing, life-changing book that it is. His insights and Zen attitude have allowed me to put this book together and take thoughts and turn them into action!

Introduction

I'll start by recognizing one undisputed fact: the world doesn't need any more self-help books. Nor does the world need another book on how to become more wealthy or healthy or wise. ***Except this book.*** This book is the distillation of decades of living and breathing its contents, of being rewarded by its magic. This book is not academic: it's succinct (no chapter is longer than one page), it's direct (easy to follow, practical advice), and it's powerful (any of these chapters can change your life right now!). Decades of reading and thinking about wealth and health, and about how the right mindset makes becoming wealthier and healthier easier. How we are all better when we are of sound mind, more wealthy, and more healthful. That's the American Dream. And this dream is available to anyone. Especially YOU!

I wrote this book because I strongly feel that you, that anyone, can become wealthy and healthy. As I like to say, you can fly like an eagle if you simply flap your arms hard enough. This book is filled with ideas and stories that could change your life, that will change your life. Skin color or education doesn't matter. In fact, nothing matters but your desire to lead a successful life. If you really want wealth and health you can and will make it happen! You may not be as smart as somebody else, but that simply means you work harder! You may not have the same education or financial resources as someone else, but that too simply means you work harder, practice discipline, and be a person of action! America is a wonderful country where there is upward mobility and freedom of choice, which means you can be wealthy and healthy if you think and act and move and grind and connect with the essential you of being wealthy and healthy!

This book is divided into three sections: mindset, wealth, and health. The mindset section is really the foundation, the Zen of personal growth. The proper mindset supports us while on our quest for wealth and health. Shorter sections on how to create real, lasting wealth and health follow. But there is no need to read this book from front to back. In fact, I discourage it! If you simply open this book to any page you may find something that resonates with you. I'm hopeful that luck and intuition will guide you to a page that will influence your life in a big way!

Personal responsibility, PR, is the major theme of this book, as PR is the foundation of everyone's success in life. I sincerely hope that *A Viking's Guide to Wealth and Health* makes a huge difference in your life and that YOU make the changes necessary to propel yourself to be the person you want to be.

An aside: although this book makes no mention of Vikings apart from the title, I think *A Viking's Guide to Wealth and Health* is a great name for this book. I am Norwegian. The Vikings are my ancestors. Think what you will about the Vikings' methods, but they made it happen. The Vikings persevered and they relied on their own strength and intuition to sail to and settle in far-off lands. You can use these same strengths (discipline, intuition, perseverance, and action) to go out and change your life today!

Pillar I – Mindset

Take responsibility. Take small steps.
Take action.

Discipline + Consistency + Time =
All of your dreams coming true.

Mindset Section Overview:

Having the proper mindset makes it so much easier to become wealthy and healthy, to live a good life. In this book, mindset simply refers to how you approach issues and tasks, specifically relating to your thoughts and actions - essentially how you see yourself and how you exist in the world. The mindset material is so powerful that just one resonating chapter will change your life!

The main components of mindset are that you have to take personal responsibly for your life, that you need to take small steps to create big change, and that you need to take action! Action action action is what it's all about. Action can range from changing how you think about relationships to taking a walk around the block every day, no matter what. When combined with grit, drive, and determination, small amounts of action over time can accomplish anything.

But first you also have to dream big! You have to dream it before you can see it, before you can want it, before you can do it. There's a golf saying that the most important muscle in golf is between your ears. In other words, your thinking and approach to the game determines the quality of your play. Understanding that all high-performance people are dreamers is a critical element to being successful. Maybe dreaming of a fabulous golf swing is the best practice you can do, yes? Start dreaming and take action. That's what it's all about.

If you're not happy with where things are, change your actions!

All actions first start as a thought. You have the ability to control your thoughts and self-talk, the ability to program yourself. Think about what you want, program in some positive self-talk and take action! *Your thoughts and actions **today** create your tomorrow.*

One thought or action today will change the rest of your life. Five push-ups, $10 saved, being nice to your sweetheart. All of these actions today affect the future. **Today** is simply a path on the way to that future. It's simple - change your thoughts and actions and change your life!

"It's not my fault!"

"It's not my fault" are the words of a loser. Blaming someone else for what happens in your life, having a victim's mentality, is what losers do. Taking personal responsibility for your actions and the results of those actions are what winners do. We call that PR - personal responsibility. Make your choice: winner or loser? This is a fundamental decision that we make in our lives. Some people never figure it out. What do you choose?

Things get better in small increments.

The idea that *things get better in small increments* means you work on new areas of self-improvement in small, manageable bites. One step at a time. Becoming fit starts with a few sit-ups every day. Becoming more financially secure starts with saving a few dollars a day, a few dollars a week.

You do not have to paint the whole house today. Just paint the south-facing side. You're not going to be able to run a marathon tomorrow, but with regular training you could sooner than you think. Do not let big tasks or goals slow you down or stop you. Instead, just take a little bite of the task. ***One by one it will be done.*** One little regular, consistent bite at a time is how we become successful, healthy, happy. Yahoo, it's up to you!

Stick with it.

Stick with it. These are words to live by. I can't tell you how many people quit before they finish. I'm going to lose fifteen pounds. I'm going to save my money. I'm going to be just a great guy at work. I'm not going to butt in when people talk.

It takes *courage* to stick with it. Sticking with it is a mindset, a way or being. Your positive self-talk will help you achieve this attitude and habit, this *mindset*. And you develop more courage every day you stick with something.

Sticking with it can be as simple as flossing your teeth, or bringing your lunch to work, or walking around the block, or saving $10.00 per week. You can do it. And when you learn to stick with it, when you learn you can do it, your whole life will be transformed!

Being a person of action **starts** with one small step, one action.

Being a person of action is a habit. But it doesn't have to start with big action; you can start with small actions. Hey, the garbage needs to go out. Boom - you do it right away. Oh, I need to call Fred back. Boom - you call him right back. If you are aware and always trying to be a person of action, to act quickly, you will create a habit of quick action and this habit will support you and care for you and make you stronger and wealthier. Yahoo!

There is a big difference between saying I can't have something versus I choose not to have something.

There is personal power in your choices. When you tell yourself (via your self-talk) that you can't have something, you are sending the "I am weak" message to yourself. The message is one of scarcity, but we know the world is full of abundance! Take charge and be strong - send the "I am strong" message to yourself instead. Send yourself the message that you have a choice.

In an effort to be healthy, I choose to avoid certain foods and I choose to eat others. I never use the language of can't, that I can't have or eat something. What I say is that I choose not to eat something.

For example, this morning with breakfast I chose not to have hash browns. The waitress said, "Oh you can't have hash browns if you're on low-carb da-de-da." I said, "Yes I can, but I choose not to." These words make you more powerful and they give you a better understanding of how your words program you and how your words have power. Use your power wisely.

What's the downside?

The concept of "what is the downside?" is critical to many areas of your life. Think of health. For food, what's the downside to eating more broccoli? What's the downside to eating more fresh fruits and vegetables? What's the downside to eating organic? Think about financially. What's the downside to saving 5% of your take-home pay? 10% of your take-home pay? What's the downside to being a little nicer to the people you work with? What's the downside to keeping your car clean? This concept allows you to make decisions quickly and easily. There is a huge downside to driving 100 MPH, but no downside to having salad for dinner.

Many times people need irrefutable proof. They need a double-blind study before eating more broccoli. But that's ridiculous. You know by looking at your friends or other people you see on the street that eating better food is healthier for you. What's the downside? Good question- and the question is the answer!

Your actions and decisions today affect the rest of your life.

It's true - today's thoughts and actions affect the rest of your life. You can look at this as good news or bad news. I look at it as good news because it means *you can change your future by changing your thoughts and actions today.* Understanding this concept is an absolute game-changer. Using self-awareness, look at your thoughts and actions right now, are they serving you well? You can improve your life right now by have more positive thoughts and taking more purposeful actions. With this mindset, you are sailing your own chosen course instead of being blown around by life. How wonderful is that!

The moment you believe you can't, you won't!

If you think you can do something, you have a better chance of getting it done! If you think you can't get it done, you certainly won't be able to do it.

All high-performance people visualize themselves succeeding. Making the shot, closing the deal. Believe in yourself. ***Believe in your ability to do whatever your heart desires.*** Visualize yourself succeeding. The foundational piece here is your self-talk. You can control your self-talk and you can tell yourself that you can do it! Because if you believe you can do it, you can!

Personal growth has four main components.

The four main components of personal growth are:

1. *Over time, any consistent effort produces big results*. Discipline + Consistency + Time = Big Results! Five push-ups every day is way better that twenty-five push-ups once in a while;

2. *Start small*. Don't try to do it all at once. If you try to do too much, you may get discouraged and quit. Starting small helps you to be consistent with your actions;

3. *Stick with it*. Failure makes you smarter, so get up and do it again. When you understand that all high-performance people have failed (most many times), you learn to focus on the "getting up and dusting yourself off" part of failure;

4. *Read books*. Successful people read books. Regularly take the time to read non-fiction. In particular, read biographies and get motivated to be successful!

Being content is wonderful!

You can be content if you choose to be content. Contentment is a choice, and that choice is up to you. If you choose to be content, life is so much smoother. Being content does not mean you don't have dreams, hopes, and aspirations. **Being content simply means to *be happy now.*** If you say, "I will be happy when I ..." then you are programming yourself to be not happy now, to be not content now. Self-programming is critical. Positive self-talk is the anecdote to negative self-programming. "I am happy now" is a great mantra.

If you choose to look across the street at the Joneses' beautiful, fancy car and become envious, that's not so content. If you are jealous of the Joneses' vacations or the new swimming pool they put in their backyard, that's not so content. Be happy where you are and understand that your happiness, your contentment, is your choice. Choose contentment and you'll be the wisest person on the block.

Listen to your intuition. Listen to that gut feeling.

Your intuition (the Universe or God) speaks first and softly. Your ego speaks second and loudly. Your intuition may softly say: careful, you have had enough to drink. Your ego may say: another drink is OK; you are a good drunk driver.

Listen to your intuition. If you're looking for a roommate and you have a gut feeling that this person would not be a good roommate, listen well, because your gut, your intuition, is speaking to you. This understanding of a loud ego voice and a soft quiet intuition is the foundation of discernment. Be a discerning listener to your intuition. ***The more you listen to your intuition the more it will speak to you***, and you'll be able to make better decisions and choices based on those feelings. I promise!

A lot of people spend their lives "getting ready to get ready."

What a great phrase. Just say the words and you totally get it. Visualize, plan, act. That's a great way to move forward. But sometimes you just have to act instead of plan and analyze, otherwise you never get it done! **Sometimes you just need to be a person of action**, because all successful people take action! Kicksumass Today!

Choose to be happy.

Our happiness is a choice, so choose to be happy. Many people do not understand their self-talk and how it affects their world. They grumble to themselves that it's raining, that it's cold, that they don't have enough money. Whatever! Stop grumbling and put a positive spin on everything you think about. It's such a wonderful way to live, being happy and positive. You will find people want to be around you. You will attract positive people into your orbit. And life will be sweeter and happier. It's easy. Choose to be happy.

Each of us has wings, but only dreamers learn to fly.

Dreaming is the tool that allows you to fly. The whole world is out there and available to you. All you have to do is dream it up. If you dream it you will be able to see it (in your mind's eye), and if you see it and believe it then it will happen. Focus on your dreams, then take action. Dreams then action! Dreams then action! While each of us has wings, only dreamers learn to fly.

What role did I play?

Your boyfriend dumps you; you have a car accident; you lose your job; you get a promotion: *what role did you play in any of those events?* We always play a role in everything that happens to us. Figure out what role you played in any outcome and be responsible for your actions that led to the outcome. **Always think about PR (personal responsibility).** If you look at what role you played, you become more personally responsible and less of a victim. You take ownership and responsibility for your life. When you have personal responsibility, you will view your thoughts and actions more carefully, realizing that those thoughts and actions are creating your future! Victims are losers; people with personal responsibility are winners! Be a winner.

Dare to be great;
Dare to live large and be somebody.

You have the ability to go out there in the world and just knock their socks off. Being successful starts with your thoughts and actions, one little step at a time. Dream big and then act, act, act, act!

The key to success is to take quality, consistent, incremental action towards your goal. If you want to own a bunch of real estate and collect passive income, start with that first house. Start with renting out your garage. But just start and Kicksumass Today!

Go the extra mile!

Go the extra mile! There is no downside to doing a little more. Start a little earlier, do a little better job, be more personable. When you go the extra mile, you will be rewarded in ways you cannot fathom. So be extra friendly to your coworker. Do a little extra work. Study a little harder. **Go the extra mile in your fitness, relationships, and personal growth.** Be active in your life and just do a little more than is required. This technique, this mindset, will increase your chances of success!

Adversity is good.

Events are neutral. You get to label them good or bad. But the idea of adversity is a good thing! Adversity builds character. Adversity demands creativity. Adversity requires a different way of looking at the world.

Throughout our lives, we are going to experience adversity. It's not a question of whether there is adversity; it's a question of how we handle it. **Adversity builds grit. Grit builds a positive, powerful person. Positive, powerful people are successful.** Think of the guy who walks out and sees his car has a flat tire. He chooses a positive label in the face of adversity and says, "Gee, I am glad the other three have air." He puts on the spare and drives to work and is powerful! Adversity is good. Don't avoid it just because it is hard.

Small changes can yield big results!

Changing small things in your life can yield big results. Having one alcoholic beverage in the evening instead of two can yield big results. Doing a small workout every morning before going to work can yield big results. Changing up what you eat in a small, easy way can yield big results. For example, always have a salad with dinner. Eating one meal that contains fresh and raw vegetables and fruits will yield big results.

Find small things to change because it's easier than big, sweeping changes. A ***key component here is for you to figure out what small change to make today.*** The figuring out gives you power and personal responsibility. A small change is not a big deal, it's not a huge lifestyle change. But small, little changes will become big game-changers over time. How fabulous is that!

Every decision you make determines your life.

Each decision you make creates a fork that determines (and changes!) your life. Left or right? A or B? Do I study tonight? Do I drink? Do I hang with my friends? Do I sharpen my axe? To a certain extent, it's hard to wrap your head around this concept. But once you buy into the concept you will pay more attention to all the decisions you make AND your life will be launched into orbit!

Each of these choices changes your life irrevocably one way or the other. So every left or right you make changes your life. It's important to understand this and then applaud all of the decisions you make. Yahoo, it's up to you!

Get in the game.

There's the old story about the fellow who is praying, "Oh dear God, oh Lord, oh God I hope I win the lottery, oh please please please let me win the lottery." All of a sudden a voice comes out of the heavens, and in a deep rumble God says, "Maybe, but first you must buy a lottery ticket."

You think you want to be rich, you think you want to be happy, you think you want Sally to go out with you, but in order for any of those things to happen, you've got to *Get in the Game!* You can't paddle a boat without oars! So take action, be a person of action, and get in the game. Buy a lottery ticket if you want to win the lottery!

Where does your ego (self-esteem) come from?

If you notice that it's important for you to have a fancy car or expensive clothes or a pretty husband or a pretty wife, then your ego is involved. But the secret is you get to choose where your ego comes from. ***You get to choose what makes you cool.***

I would rather have money in the bank than a fancy car or a big house. My money in the bank makes me cool (Note: I have created my own mindset). I would rather have a healthy body and a healthy mind than a Rolex watch or a luxury vacation. My health makes me cool. ***Look at yourself introspectively and figure out what boosts your ego.*** If the ego hit comes from a place that is shallow and does not serve you, change your hot button - that is, change what boosts your ego.

Remember that ***what you focus on expands*** (AND you get to choose what to focus on), so focus on how great it is to be healthy. Focus on how great it is to have money in the bank. Focus on how great it is to have some lovely flowers in your kitchen. ***Use your self-talk to help you focus*** on what you want and who you want to be, and to change your hot buttons to be in line with these desires. You'll be less reactive and envious, and more intentional and appreciative. How great is that!

Whatever you do, it gets easier the more you do it.

Think about the best way to start doing push-ups. Begin with one push-up. Do one push-up every day for a week. Then two. Pretty soon three, four, five, six, seven, eight, nine, ten! Doing push-ups gets quite a bit easier the more you do them. This is true for everything we do in life. Una metáfora!

Talking sincerely to your sweetheart. Having a difficult business conversation. Learning to stand up in front of an audience and speak articulately. It gets easier the more you do it. It's almost magical! If you just swim your laps you'll become a better swimmer, but the key is to swim the laps. So be a person of action and get after it!

Over time, small things make a big difference.

Brewing your coffee at home every day and saving $4 a day, $5 a day, $10 a day makes a huge difference over thirty years. *Ten dollars per day for 30 years @ 6% interest turns out to be $301,354.* WOW! It starts one day at a time, one action at a time. This is true for everything. If you do five push-ups every day, pretty soon you'll be a lot stronger. Pretty soon you'll be up to six, seven, eight, nine, ten push-ups. Choose goals that are easy to attain and stick with them. This is how you achieve long-term change. *Regular and consistent small actions* adding up to big changes over time!

Focus is a law of attraction.

If you focus on something you want to attract, you'll have a better chance of attracting it to you. When you focus on who you want to be, those qualities will be drawn from your inner depths and become you. Whatever you want will be drawn to you through your focus on it.

Remember: ***What you focus on Expands.*** If you focus on good luck, if you focus on good health, if you focus on love, all of those things will come into your life. Use your self-talk to help you focus on what you want and who you want to be. That's the law of attraction.

Don't blame anyone else for your position in life.

Your financial position, your health, your relationships - it's all up to you. If you say things like "Oh, they don't pay me enough," or "Oh, the prices have gone up so much, I can't afford a house," or "I just can't; it's too difficult," you're making the comments of a loser.

Be a winner and take charge. Take responsibility. Do what it takes to save money, to get healthy, to eat better. Do what it takes to do whatever you want. PR equals personal responsibility. If you exhibit personal responsibility in your world, life gets smoother because you are in charge (of your thoughts and actions). Take charge of yourself today!

They don't pay me enough.

These words are not helpful. If you're not making as much money as you would like, *figure out* how to make more money. Everyone generally wants to make more money! Does it take more education or training? Does it take changing jobs? Does it take you *figuring out* how to be more valuable for your employer? If you can learn to **figure stuff out** you will be way more successful at everything! If you're not making enough money, do you have the guts and the smarts to start your own business? "They don't pay me enough" gives your power away, it makes you weak and ineffectual. PR means personal responsibility. If you want more money, *figure out* how to get it. Yahoo, it's up to you!

Be present.

This may sound like odd advice, but be present when you're reading a book, doing your homework, or watching TV. Multitasking is overrated. Avoid multitasking and do one thing at a time. ***When you wash the dishes, wash the dishes.*** Nothing else. Focus on that one thing and do it well, with intention through presence. Yes, even when watching TV. Pay attention to the dialogue, the plot, the setting - immerse and enjoy. When reading a magazine or a book, pay attention to those words - turn off the music or TV in the background and be present and attune to what the book or magazine has to say to you. When you listen to someone, don't think of your reply. Hear their words, their pattern of speech, their emotion. ***Meditative listening.*** Learning how to be present is a wonderful tool and a wonderful gift to all friends and family that you interact with. And it's a true gift to yourself and those things you wish to learn. So be present - and when you wash the dishes, wash the dishes.

Who has your ear?
Who is the influence in your life?

What an interesting concept. Who do you listen to? Who has your ear? What books do you read? Who do you hang with? What is your significant other whispering to you? If you're hanging with losers and big spenders, they have your ear just because you're hanging around them. Hang with winners. Hang with savers. Hang with healthy people. ***You will move towards and become like those who have your ear.*** Listen wisely.

The more you focus on the bright side of things, the brighter it gets!

Remember: *What you focus on Expands*. And if you focus on the bright side, if you focus on the positive, if you focus on the optimistic, your life gets brighter, more positive, and more optimistic. It's a no brainer. **If you think and talk about positive stuff, everything around you becomes more positive and fun!** By setting your thoughts to the "positive bright side," your entire world brightens (and lightens) up!

Don't give up on your **dreams**.

How are you going to have a dream come true unless you have a dream! Figure out what your dreams are, and then work and claw and work some more until your dreams come true. Focus on it. Figure it out. Think about it. Daydream. Visualize.

Remember that many of your dreams won't turn into reality tomorrow. You have to take many small, manageable positive steps to get there. Step by step you are creating a better you. The key is to take the steps. ***The key is to take action.*** The key is to keep your eyes on the prize. Do whatever it takes to make that dream come true! If you want to become a real estate mogul, start today with one small real estate investment. Do something today to move your dreams closer to reality!

Be happy today.

Being happy will allow you to attract other happy, positive people into your life. When you're happy, you have more love, more energy and more good things happening to you. You will attract positive things to yourself. And happiness can also make you wealthier. Frankly, you'll make more money because happy people are way more likely to get that better job, to get that promotion, to start that business, to be successful. So put a positive spin on life. Choose to be happy, and the universe will reward your efforts.

The path.

A path is simply a symbol for the steps someone has taken before you. In nearly all of your endeavors, people have made a path or illuminated the way. The path shows you how they did it and it informs you how to get where you want to go. For most of our endeavors, there are books written by successful people willing to show you the path to success. It takes effort to find the right book or author and the path they recommend, but once you find it, follow it!

In athletics, there's a lot of information about how to train, how to work on your mental game, how to recover faster. In sports, health, or wealth you do not have to reinvent the wheel, you simply need to find a path. *One way to find a path is to develop relationships with mentors.* Often an older and more experienced person will be willing to help you and share his or her experience with someone trying to find their way. Take advantage of that. It's a shortcut to getting on the right path! *Another way to figure out the path is to read books.* There are tons of self-help and instructional books. And remember: successful people read books.

It all starts with desire.

Whether you want health, wealth, physical fitness, or a better relationship, it all starts with desire. If you really, really, really want something, then you will figure out a way to get it. And the more you focus on it, the more of it will happen. But desire is the key. Whether you want to get rid of your tummy, stand up taller, have a better retirement, you have to start with desire - you have to want it!

And sure, you need to lay out a plan and take little steps to achieve what you want, but desire will bring you there. Guaranteed! All you have to do is want it, think about it, and take action on it!

I suggest you read *Think and Grow Rich* by Napoleon Hill. Written many years ago, it sold millions of copies. It's the granddaddy of much of my thinking about these things. He wrote that the common thread weaving together successful people is desire! This isn't just talking about money. It's about being a good artist. It's about being a good swimmer. It's about being more fit or being a better parent. If you really, really, really, really want it, it's guaranteed. Think about it and act, and it will happen automatically. Now go out there and get after it!

Change means opportunity.

Sometimes the older we get the less we like change. When we understand that change is constant and that change can create opportunity, then we can choose to view change as a positive! Opportunity is good. Opportunity is the industrial revolution. Opportunity is the PC Revolution. Opportunity is artificial intelligence. Don't be afraid of the future. Embrace it. *Allow change to be your friend.* A positive attitude regarding change feels good and puts you in a position to take advantage of change. Get ready!

The more stuff you have the less free you are.

Believe it or not, the more stuff you have - boats, cars, planes, houses, jet skis, artwork, clothes - the less free you are. All of that stuff takes time and attention. All of that stuff causes you to be chained to your possessions. All of that stuff causes you to have to worry about taking care of it. It causes you to pay for taking care of it, for insurance, for storage. It's a total brain and money drain.

On the other hand, being a minimalist is pretty sweet. It conserves your money and it also allows you to lead a simpler, more rewarding life. **Often, simpler is better.** For example, a friend and a past bookkeeper always gave away any clothes that she had not worn in one year. She was allowing the love and energy to flow through her life, while staying minimal. Good idea, yes?

Hang out with positive, like-minded people.

The people you hang out and associate with make a huge difference in your life. Choose to hang out with people who are positive, who are winners, who are ethical, and who are enthusiastic. These people are so much more fun to hang out with! Remember you get to choose who you hang with!

If you go to a party and there's a bunch of negative losers there, you will be negatively influenced by just being in their presence - even if you don't talk to them. Negative energy is as infectious as positive energy. Your choice to be at a party with negative folks is a choice that impacts you.

Look at your friends and think about who among them are positive, loving, and supportive, and choose to hang out with them. Dump the losers and stick with the winners. This is not a passive activity - you get to choose your friends. Choose like-minded positive friends to hang out with, and let the negative people in your life fall by the wayside. It may be painful at first, but it will pay huge dividends in the future.

Good habits are your best friend!

Good habits are truly your best friend. I was recently driving along and I knew there were no cars near me, that the lane beside me was empty. Since there were no cars near me, I knew it was OK to change lanes. But I have a habit of always looking over my shoulder before I change lanes - and holy cow there was a car there! *My good habit saved an accident.*

Grow those thoughts and actions into good habits and save yourself not just from car accidents, but from all sorts of accidents! Create the habit of thinking positive thoughts, the habit of being a good friend, the habit of saving 10% from every paycheck. Once you create (notice this is an affirmative action!) a positive habit, the habit becomes part of who you are. And then you're off to a happier and more successful life!

Choose the positive perspective.

How you label events in your life is up to you, because you get to choose how to define all that happens in your life. While vacationing, I was walking to breakfast and I noticed I had forgotten my reading glasses. I could have said, "Boy, you're so dumb. You always forget stuff." But I did not say that because I always choose the positive perspective. Instead, I said, "Gosh, I'm glad I remembered when I was only halfway there! Man you have a great memory. You remembered. Good work, John." Choose the positive perspective and you'll develop a wonderful habit that will build you up and make you strong. Your world will become brighter, smoother, and richer. How's that for positive thinking?

If you can dream it, you can do it!

All high-performance people visualize their future actions. If you can dream it, you can do it, so dream big! Visualize yourself making the baseball team. Visualize yourself fit and healthy. Visualize yourself being wildly successful. Visualize all the details of your success: the people you will hang with, the actions you will take, how you will look and walk and think and present. Visualizing is active and you can do it on purpose. When you wake up, you can picture or visualize how your day is going to go, and many times what you visualize happens! If you picture it in your mind, you will be inextricably drawn toward the picture. I'm telling you it works - and it's so powerful. So dream big today!

Preset your attitude.

If you preset your attitude to positive (seriously you can do this), many things that occur during your day will be positive! Have you ever noticed when you're in a new city, where you think the food is going to be so good and the people so friendly, that the food ends up being so good and the people so friendly? I'm not sure whether you'll just be drawn to the right restaurant or if they'll just serve you the right food, but it really works. ***Preset your attitude to positive, loving, affirming, and all of those good things will come your way.*** The first step is always to smile. This is an active choice. You preset your attitude on purpose. It is like forethought - plan on having a great time and it usually happens!

Hard work beats talent when talent does not work hard!

It's all about hard work. Focus on the goal and work like a dog. Hard work beats talent every time. The world is filled with lazy, talented people. You can make it happen simply by working hard. There are always people smarter and better connected than you. **But no one works harder than you.** Out work the competition. No matter what it takes, do what it takes! Working hard means working smart. Working hard means putting in the time. And if you work really hard, you will have a much better chance at being successful!

Just change one small thing at a time to increase your odds of success.

Keep it easy. Keep it simple. If you make it too hard you won't do it. Everyone has New Year's resolutions: I'm going to do 50 push-ups a day. I'm going to lose 70 pounds. I'm never going to have dessert again. These are hard changes and most folks do not follow through! The key here is to make small promises to yourself, and **absolutely** *keep your promises.* Be consistent with your actions. 5 push-ups a day, every day, for years, is way better than starting with 50 push-ups for a few days then quitting.

If you keep it simple, if you keep it easy, you will be much more likely to continue with the change. How about doing three push-ups every morning? How about promising to walk around the block three times a week? How about starting a savings account and saving $10 a month? All of these are really easy changes and the important part is not to quit but to keep at it. You have to be a winner and continue to keep the change alive; figure out how to keep at it. Do you make a check list on your mirror where you give yourself a gold star? Make the change a habit, then the habit will become part of your life. The key is to make it easy, easy, easy, simple, simple, simple and stay at it! Change your world one small step at a time!

Make good foundational decisions.

Living below your means is a foundation for your wealth. Eating low-calorie high-nutrition food is a foundation for your health. The foundation of any enterprise, any organization, any home, any relationship, is made up of the underlying principles of the entity. If those foundational decisions are good, your world is destined for success. *If you can notice what the foundational choices are then you will be in a better position to make a good decision.*

If you are refinancing your home and you have the option to increase your loan by $50,000 (and put $50,000 in your pocket and maybe take a big vacation) but also increase your payment, it is essential to notice this as a foundational decision that will impact your future. The key is to figure out that certain decisions are truly foundational AND look out above our headlights and see where these choices put us in the years to come.

The roadmap to success.

If we look at the qualities and characteristics of successful people and emulate those in our daily lives, we will be following the roadmap to success. We can learn from the efforts and success of others. Biographies are a great source of information about folks who are and have been successful.

Looking at a successful person: why do they arrive early at meetings; why do they return their phone calls, emails, and texts quickly; why do they look you in the eyes; why are they honest, clean, and neat; why are they organized with a plan; why are they tenacious? These are the highways and byways that make up the roadmap of success. I promise you, if you follow the roadmap you will be irrevocably driven and pulled to success!

When you think about something that needs to get done, do it right away.

"*Do it do it now*" are great words for success. Many of us postpone tasks. Knocking down dominoes, moving forward, getting things done, that's the way of a successful person. Car's dirty? Wash it. Time to do laundry? Do it. House a mess? Clean it. Get in the habit of doing it now and you'll earn huge dividends down the road. ***Do it do it now*** are words to live by. These words are a mantra for being a person of action AND all successful people are people of action! In fact, ***do it do it now*** becomes a habit, the habit of a successful person!

Hope is not a strategy for success.

Being hopeful is great, but you need to **be a Person of Action** if you want to be successful. You need to be an active thinker and doer. Getting good grades at school, having more friends, being more financially secure, reading more, having better relationships - it all takes action.

And of course it takes action to be successful. So little by little you take action. ***Remember you don't become successful in one big action; it takes many small, consistent steps to achieve success.***

If you want to be more well-read, spend an hour reading every day. If you want to have more financial literacy, read books about finances, talk to your smart pals, watch financial news. Day trade with play money. If you want to be more fit and get rid of those extra ten pounds, start walking for 1/2 hour every morning. Stretch. Do three push-ups every day.

No matter what it is, it takes action! Hoping is great, thinking about something is pretty darn good, but to really get it done you have to be a person of action.

How to be Happy.

How to be happy? The answer is very simple: you **choose to be happy**. Happiness is a choice. Just like sadness is a choice. Remember, events are neutral. It's how we categorize that event that make us happy or sad. One great way to be happy is to be grateful for all the good things in your life: focus on and be grateful for the simple things you have. Be grateful for the roof over your head, for running water, for enough food, for having a job even if it is not the best job in the world. This sets the tone for your life and it puts a smile on your face!

If you get a flat tire in the morning, are you going to be happy or sad? **Your choice**. You could be happy because you have a spare tire. You could be happy because you have two arms and two legs to install the spare tire. Or you could be sad because you have a flat tire that is an inconvenience. But what good does that do?

So choose to be happy. Happy people have more fun and have more friends AND generally make more money. Happiness is, well, happy! Why not? What a great choice. What's the downside of deciding to be happy?

People create their destiny through their choices!

Remember, every choice we make generally turns into an action (or inaction). Your thoughts and actions today create your tomorrow (even the little itty-bitty thoughts and actions). **Your destiny, who you are, is simply the sum of all your thoughts and actions**. We can create our destiny, so get on it. Yahoo!

I am going to start saving next year -
WRONG!

Start now. Let me repeat myself, start now. The time for action is now! *Successful people take action*. So start saving now, even if it's a dollar a week, $10 a week, $100 a week. It doesn't matter, just start now. Habits are created and then the habits create you, so start now.

I was just thinking about my friend who at the age of 45 decided to splurge on a fancy new house. Well, the problem is he didn't invest that money to create passive income and now he's 67 years-old and he doesn't have enough money to retire. Remember that your thoughts and action in the past determine where you are today. If he would have started saving earlier, if he would have been consistent, he would be rocking and rolling financially! He would be off to French Polynesia. **So the rule is: do it do it now**. **Do it do it now** applies to everything: your homework, eating fresh fruits and vegetables, saving your money. So just start now and you may surprise yourself how much you accomplish and how successful you can be!

You can fly like an eagle if you just flap your arms hard enough!

What I mean by this is you need to **_get in the game_** to be successful - to fly. You need to be in the game to be successful, to be healthy, to be wealthy, to have lots of friends, to have a nice yard, to have a clean car.

To get in the game means to change things up. It means to alter your behavior. Do you want to be healthy? Try not eating meat for a month. Try no alcohol for a month. Change things up. Do you want to be wealthy? Spend less and save more. Buy a rental property. Alter your behavior. There is an old saying that says you can't hit a home run from the bleachers. To be able to hit the ball you must be on the team AND on the field. Get in the game!

Learn your lesson, but from someone else's mistake!

My friend Ed had a bunch of money. He lived in a big fancy house on the golf course. He and his wife each had beautiful Mercedes. Ed put all of his money in one asset. You can guess what happened. He lost all his money when that investment went sideways. Now he's living in a mobile home in Palm Springs. What a drag.

If you put all your eggs in one basket you won't have asset allocation AND if that investment goes south you are in financial trouble! You do not have to be Ed to learn from his mistake. You can learn from Ed's mistake by just hearing about Ed's mistake. If you pay attention, you can watch someone else's actions and learn from them. Both what to and what not to do. This is a huge shortcut to success. Prime your brain to learn from others and jump-start your future.

Kicksumass today.

How good is this really! Choose to act. Choose to act decisively. Choose to go Kicksumass Today! Go out and open up a can of whoop-ass. These are all expressions talking about enthusiasm and going forward with power and love. Get up off the couch and go take action. Get up, stand up. Stand tall with your chest out and your chin up and go kicksumass. Life is waiting for you so go do it. Take action now. The critical element to our success is action. Action! When? Today! Stop planning, stop procrastinating. Start acting! All high-performance people are men of action, women of action! When? Today! Go Kicksumass Today!

You can't teach that.

You can't teach someone how to be successful from a classroom. There is a huge difference between the theory of what it takes to be successful and the practice of success. Success takes grit, guts, creativity, and persistence. You can't teach that. It's analogous to the financial consultant. If the financial consultant really knew what he was doing he would not have a job as a consultant, he would have his own jet. No matter what you hear about what it takes to be successful, remember *grit, guts, creativity, and persistence* are the most important skills you can cultivate. You learn these skills from doing, from action. To acquire these traits, you must get in the game.

Increase your chances of success!

Believe it or not, if you do two simple things your chances of success will increase dramatically! First, return your phone calls, emails, and texts instantly (just as quickly as you can). And second, show up to meetings ten or fifteen minutes early. That's it!

If you return communications quickly and show up to meetings early, you'll be known as *Mr. or Ms. Dependable*. Mr. Dependable makes more money. Ms. Dependable gets more opportunities. Ms. Dependable is more successful. Mr. Dependable is known to be on it! Think I'm joking? Recall how disrespectful it is when somebody shows up to a meeting fifteen minutes late or when someone does not call you back for several days. And you learn they're not dependable. If you return your communications promptly and show up early to your meetings, your success coefficient goes way up. Yahoo, it's up to you!

The three bones.

The three most important bones in your body are your funny bone, your wish bone, and your backbone. A *funny bone* is important because people want to hang around someone who has a sense of humor and is happy. A **wish bone** is important because we should have positive, wonderful things to look forward to in our lives. A *backbone* is important so we can stand up tall for what we believe in and so we will have the grit to do what it takes. If you cultivate these three bones, your chances of success will go way up!

Don't accept a victim mentality.

Never accept that it's somebody else's fault that you can't be successful, that you can't lose weight, that you can't make it through college. Don't accept that if you're brown, if you're fat, if you're bald, you can't be successful. Say no to the victim mentality. **Say no to *it's not my fault.***

In our society today there a lot of "victims" who won't accept responsibility for their thoughts and actions. But that's not you. *Accept responsibility.* Stand up tall and be a winner. Winners take action and accept the consequences of that action! If the actions don't work out, winners change course. But winners don't play the victim.

Pay attention to the little things.

When you pay attention to the little things, when you're grateful for the small moments in your life, your whole world is smooth and happy. When you enjoy putting on your really comfy shoes and socks in the morning. When you have a beautiful little plant in your entryway and you sit down and admire and really appreciate that fabulous plant, your whole day gets better and smoother. Find grateful moments and enjoy the little things. Your life gets better automatically. Being grateful is a positive action you can take AND people are drawn to and enjoy being around positive people!

Life is very fair.
You reap what you sow.

Think about it - you reap what you sow. What you plant, you can harvest - whether that's ideas, friendships, or business opportunities. Save your money to create passive income. When you have passive income, life is sweeter. Reap what you sow. When you work out and exercise, your body is better and you don't attract those crummy, terrible diseases. You reap what you sow. What a concept. *So again, your thoughts and actions today create tomorrow.* You reap what you sow. This is a wonderful lesson and it is a positive lesson. If you plant positive things the rewards will be positive. If you choose to be a victim (blaming other people for the results of your thoughts and actions) well... you will just be another unsuccessful victim!

Take ownership.

When you take ownership of your actions, when you take ownership of any situation, you become more powerful and you will grow from that ownership. *It's called personal responsibility (PR)*. Take ownership of the grade you receive, a review of your performance, or a mistake in a relationship. Ownership is critical to your personal growth and your success because you will be accountable to yourself.

A good question to ask yourself is "what role did I play?" *Take ownership of your role, take ownership of the outcome*. Do that, and your personal growth will be off the charts!

When the going gets tough, the **tough** get going.
Seriously!

If it were easy, everyone would do it. Sometimes you have to be tough to be successful. Sometimes you have to work hard to be successful. Sometimes you have to knock down obstacles to be successful. ***Realize that hard work and struggle are the dues you have to pay to be successful.*** Every time you struggle, you get closer to the goal. When you think about struggle as progress, you are encouraged by the struggle. Buck up and make it happen!

Put a smile on your face.

This thought may sound a little silly, but it is a very powerful action. A smile is your best greeting. When you smile at someone, they can't help but smile back. Smile and you'll make more friends and more money. I promise.

Routines are a double-edged sword.

Routines can be your friend if the habit you are creating is a good one. These are positive routines. Eating well, brushing your teeth first thing in the morning, saying thank you to your sweetie as she hands you a cup of coffee. *But some routines can be bad if they stop you from creativity, from hard work, and from personal growth*. These are negative routines such as always having a glass of wine when you get home from work or reading trashy fiction on your lunch break.

I personally love routines because they help me create positive habits. A routine allows me to grow positive habits that improve my life. I stretch and meditate every morning. I always drink a couple glasses of water to start my day. These began as routines that have led to great habits! Figure out what your positive habits are and look for more actions (or thoughts) that you can turn into positive habits.

Figure it out!

When you learn *the skill of figuring it out* you become much more useful to yourself and those around you. There is immense power in knowing that you can figure it out. And this is a skill - *the skill of applying the discipline and stick-to-itiveness, the grit and resourcefulness, that gets the job done.* And the confidence you get from knowing you can figure it out will make you more money, create richer relationships, and give you the power and responsibility to get things done. There is great personal power in this mindset. What's it going to take for you to figure it out?

Your struggles today will help you develop strength in the future.

Struggles are not bad. All of us struggle at one time or another. The little baby learning how to walk is struggling. He just doesn't know how to label it - he simply does it. Don't focus on the struggle; focus on the goal. Don't treat yourself as a victim of hardship; embrace the hardship.

Understand that the struggle is simply the path you take toward being successful and healthy. Remember, all successful people have struggled. If you haven't struggled, you haven't developed grit, and all successful people have grit. Embrace the struggle; grow with the struggle. Get gritty and get 'er done!

With freedom comes responsibility.

Generally, people associate this saying with political responsibilities; that is, with the freedom to elect officials in a democracy comes the responsibility of doing your homework and picking honest politicians.

But **with freedom comes responsibility means many things.** When your parents chose not to leave a babysitter with you for the first time, you were trusted to act responsibly. When you work for yourself, you have the freedom to sleep in or to get up early, to work late or to not work at all, but you also have the responsibility to yourself to be successful. All of us have the freedom to save or not to save, each action creating our future. Freedom and responsibility - what a concept. It's amazing that you become more powerful when you're free and *accept the responsibility* of doing the right thing, of making good decisions. Choose freedom and responsibility.

I don't have time to do any reading -
wrong!

Of course you have time to read. All you have to do is turn the television off. **Do what it takes** to spend half an hour every day reading good nonfiction - history, politics, self-improvement - anything, so long as it's quality. I love reading biographies. They inspire me!

It is a good habit to schedule reading on your calendar. Look at your schedule, figure out where your time goes, and determine when you can you sit down and do some reading. Whether it's after dinner or before work, **do what it takes** to spend half an hour reading every day. Do that, and your personal growth will be off the charts! And it is worth noting that "**do what it takes**" is a very powerful thought!

You have two ears and one mouth for a reason.

Many of us are good talkers but poor listeners. And we certainly know folks who don't listen at all. We all have the experience of "listening" to someone talk, but instead of really listening we are formulating our answer to their statements. That's not listening.

Try to give someone your undivided attention when they're speaking (this is respectful listening and they will notice YOU paying attention). Focus on their words, not your response to those words. ***Mindful listening is a gift to the other person***, a gift they may not be aware that you're giving them, but a gift all the same. So listen with both ears, not your mouth. God gave us two ears and one mouth, and we should use them in that proportion. Listen twice and talk once.

Rise to the occasion!

Life happens. And no matter what happens, you have two choices: you can take ownership and rise to the occasion or you can be a victim and blame someone else.

Losers play the victim; winners take ownership - it's called PR – personal responsibility. Losers sit on the couch and wonder what happened. Winners figure it out and move forward. Rising to the occasion means taking responsibility for your part in whatever happens in your life. If your girlfriend leaves you, it's not all her fault (if you blame her you are playing victim). You had some role in her leaving, so stand up tall and take personal responsibility.

When life happens, when you get wet in a rainstorm, when you're tired and just want to stop working, running, studying, rise to the occasion, be personally responsible, and do what it takes to be successful. People who rise to the occasion have grit and grit is necessary for personal growth and success. Rise up and stand tall!

The message from Batman applies to your whole life!

"The reason you fall is so you can learn to pick yourself up." What a powerful message! We stumble so we can catch our balance. We fall down, but we always get back up. That's what life is about. If you feel sorry for yourself or play victim then you don't learn that lesson. Getting back up and being stronger and smarter is a common trait of successful people.

It's wonderful when you lose money in a deal, when you get fired from your job, when you gain a little weight, when you do not make the team. All of these events are ***opportunities for you to dust yourself off, stand up tall, and powerfully move forward.*** Learning to get up after you fall is one of the key ingredients to being successful in any area of life. Prepare to fall (everyone does), but be ready to get right back up!

<u>NOTES</u>

Pillar II – Wealth

How to save money and put that money to work building a future where your money works for you, rather than you working for your money.

Wealth Section Overview:

I'll be honest with you: you can become wealthy if you really want to…there's no secret recipe, no magic spell. Just simple steps. One step, then another. This section provides step-by-step actions that will allow you to become wealthy. No question about it. While there are many rules to follow to help you become wealthy, the big takeaway is to spend less than you earn, save your money, and invest that money in assets that create passive income. That's it. It's what I've done for as long as I can remember, and it's THE reason I'm wealthy.

There are many roadmaps and hints in these chapters. If you simply follow one of them, it will change your life. For example: save 10% of your take-home pay. Right off the bat. No matter what. If you immediately bank 10% of your net pay, your financial world will change forever!

I know you'll enjoy this section - it's near and dear to my heart and I personally have learned many of these rules and lessons the hard way. Being wealthy is not a goal in and of itself, but it's a facilitator for an enjoyable and secure life. And that's one goal we all work towards, even if we think we've already have obtained it.

Can you save $5 per day?

If you can simply save $5 each and every day, at the end of twenty years you will have saved $69,306 (assuming 6% gain per year). Save $5 per day and in thirty years you will have $150,677! Yahoo! It is basically found money. Absolutely amazing. This is the power of compound interest, perseverance, and the beauty of creating a good habit. And the wonderful thing is if you figure out how to save $5 per day, you will be able to figure out how to save $10 or $20 per day! Then we're talking serious dollars. Make good decisions early and watch that money grow! Your future is up to you!

Buying a used car versus a new car.

You have $10,000 saved for a down payment on a new car. Let's look at the difference between borrowing an additional $40,000 to buy a fancy new car versus using that $10,000 to buy a used car. I'll do the math for you.

$10,000 you spend either way. To buy that fancy car, you need to borrow an additional $40,000 payable over 84 months at 4% interest. At those terms, the monthly payment will be $546.75. After interest, you are really borrowing about $46,000.

Keep those numbers in your mind. Instead of buying a new car, you decide to buy a used car and forgo borrowing any money. And you decide to take the amount of the car payment ($546.75) and invest it at the same interest rate (4%) that you're paying for your new car. That is, you are earning 4% on your money rather than paying 4% to borrow money.

If you invest $546.75 per month for 84 months with a 4% return, you will have nearly $53,000 in the bank at the end of seven years, having earned about $7,000 in interest (rather than paying about $6,000 in interest). It's essentially a $100,000 swing. You've put $53,000 in your pocket instead of spending $46,000. That's a lot of money!

If you were to bank the money rather than buy a new car you will feel good about yourself. More importantly, you're not just stupidly playing the Keep Up with The Joneses game. Smart! Get some jingle in your jeans and stand up tall because you my friend have made a really great choice. Be proud - be a saver!

Beware of the big Cash-Flow Trap!

The Cash-Flow Trap is the illusion that just because you have big cash flow you think you're rich. But big cash flow does not mean you are rich. Big cash flow means that you have lots of money flowing through (and out of!) your bank account, but unless you've invested it well, you may not have any real assets. You may not even have any money in the bank. So you may have big Cash Flow, but you may also fall into the trap of living a lifestyle that needs all that cash flow. That's gotta stop!

So big Cash Flow gives you two choices: you can either spend all your cash flow on stuff (new houses, cars, clothes, jewelry) or you can save it and create passive income. Remember passive income is the goal! Give yourself freedom and choose to invest that big cash flow rather than just spending it away.

"What are you doing?"

When I was a young man, I watched as my friend hunched over his checkbook. I said, "Craig, what are you doing?" He said, "I'm going through my checkbook figuring out what expenses are unnecessary." What a concept! I had no idea what Craig was doing, but he was reducing his burn rate. He was finding expenses that were unnecessary and cutting them out. What a move!

The first step to creating passive income is having enough money to invest. This requires spending less than you make, which means you can do two things: spend less AND make more. Do both, and people will ask you, "What are you doing?"

Hints on how to save money.

For most people, their two biggest expenses are for housing and transportation. The key to saving on these expenses is simple. Don't spend a lot on your house; don't spend a lot on your car. One idea is to bring in a roommate and share the costs. Maybe live at home with your parents for a few years and bank it hard. Get rid of the car payment and drive a used car or take the bus. Be smart - make it a game. Reduce these costs as much as possible and you'll have more money to put in your savings account. Maybe when you buy a house look for a daylight basement so you can create a "mother-in-law" apartment and create passive income.

A savings account gives you freedom (**MIF = Money is Freedom**). A savings account gives you money to invest in passive income-earning assets. Money in the bank allows you to work less when you're older and have more fun. Money in the bank gives you security and allows you to take better care of your family. Make sense?

Spend slowly; save quickly.

Spend Slowly. Save Quickly. Use these words as your game plan, as your mantra. *Slow down when you're spending money.* There's no rush to spend. But feel free to *speed up when you're saving money.* The result of this thought shift is your whole modus operandi changes. Hold on, do we really need this? Let's put a little more money in savings.

It makes such a big difference if you can save an extra $10 or $100 per week. Remember, *what you focus on expands*. If you're focused on all the stuff you want, then you'll spend more money on all of those things. If you're thinking about and focusing on your savings and your passive income, that will grow almost all by itself. **Spend slowly. Save quickly**. These are words to live by!

Pay **yourself** first.

One easy way to save money: when you get your paycheck, the first person you pay is yourself. That's right - pay yourself first! Take at least 10% of your take-home pay and put it in a savings account. In fact, open up a new savings account and call it the Pay Me First account. The BEST way to make sure you pay yourself first is to set up an automatic transfer (this is critically important AND the key to savings) to this special savings account!

If you *pay yourself first each and every payday*, pretty soon you'll have a substantial amount of money in your new bank account. Do not touch that money until you are ready to use it to invest in passive income-producing assets.

Remember, if you take care of your pennies, your dollars will take care of themselves. This may be old-fashioned advice, but it's old-fashioned advice that can really pay off! So pay yourself first, sock that money away, and watch it grow!

I just saved $3.00!

Wasting your money makes it more difficult to have assets that create passive income. My sweetie and I went out for dinner and we ordered two waters. They brought bottled water and wanted to charge me $1.50 each. I ordered tap water and saved three bucks. A penny saved is a penny earned might sound trite, but it's a big deal.

And this is significant because many of my friends would not bother with a $3.00 expense. Interestingly, the ones who would not bother are not as financially sound as I am. My choices have put me in a wonderful position! In fact, the year this happened I personally made over a million dollars! So why would I bother? Because watching my pennies is a habit and I value not being wasteful!

The 5/10/20/40 real estate rule.

Hold good income-producing real estate for 5 years and you will see that you were smart to buy it. Own income-producing real estate for 10 years and you were really damn smart to buy it. Own income-producing real estate for 20 years and it's clear you're a freaking genius. Hold it for 40 years and you're like my friend Sven who bought a commercial property 40 years ago for $100,000 and recently sold it for $8 Million!

One key to generating passive income is to put time on your side. Own real estate, and let your tenants pay the mortgage for you. Once that mortgage is paid off, most of the rent goes in your pocket. Plus, you should be able to sit back and watch as the real estate appreciates. It's a double win!

How do I live below my means?

There are three main steps to living below your means:

1. *Pay yourself first.* That's right, pay yourself first. When you get your paycheck, the first person you pay is yourself. Take at least 10% of your take-home pay and put that money in a separate account that you do not touch. Set up an automatic transfer into your savings account so you don't have to think about transferring the money (*this is key*). If you do that each and every payday, pretty soon you'll have a substantial amount of money. Remember, if you take care of your pennies your dollars will take care of themselves. It works little by little, but eventually your passive income will be more than your paycheck!

2. *Reduce your cash burn.* The less you spend the more you'll have to save, so cut out all unnecessary expenses. There are easy expenses to cut out - $4 lattes (that's a good car every ten years!), extra cable channels, car washes, eating out. There are hard lifestyle choices you need to make now so you can live well later - selling your car and taking public transportation, living in a smaller apartment than you can afford, buying used clothes and furniture. You know that old saying about keeping up with the Joneses. Well, only keep up with the Joneses if they are savers!

3. *It's not about what you make; it's about what you save.* It does not matter what you make on a weekly or monthly basis. All that matters is to figure out how you can live below your means and put some money in the bank. Some people say, "I don't make enough to save." *Not true.* What you need to do is spend less and bank more. Pretty simple and it always works!

Focus on having money instead of looking like you have money.

Focusing on fancy stuff steals your focus and your money. You don't want to focus on what money can buy you because spending money to show off diminishes your ability to create passive income (and it's monumentally stupid!).

Focus on saving and creating wealth, having money and creating passive income. Remember, *what we focus on expands*, so if you focus on all of the things money can buy: the cool clothes, the fancy car, the luxury trips, that's what you'll start to care about. So focus on actually having money in the bank, rather than the accoutrements of money. Because it's way better to have money than to look like you have money.

Seriously, pay yourself first!

Ok, I'll say it again. It's that important. As soon as you get your paycheck, put at least 10% of it in a segregated savings account. Remember that good habits are your friend, so get in the habit of paying yourself first! And set the intention of having that money grow. That is, do not touch it! Set your account up so you *automatically transfer* the money into your passive income savings account. You will never even notice it is not there AND your savings will grow!

You can always find reasons to spend your money: we need a new car; we need a new washer; we need new furniture. But be stronger than the urge to spend, and let the automatic transfer outsmart yourself (really). I'm not saying it's easy, but winners do what it takes to be successful, so be a winner! Pay yourself first and watch the savings grow!

Deferred gratification helps you really appreciate something when you buy it.

Deferred gratification is a wonderful thing. Deferred gratification sets you apart from the crowd. Deferred gratification helps you slow down your purchasing and speed up your savings.

If you make yourself wait to buy something, not only will you really think hard about whether you should buy it, but you also get the pleasure of anticipation. Anticipation is half the payoff of buying or doing something. Anticipating travel, imagining getting on the airplane and the joy of takeoff is half the fun! Anticipating that new car. Anticipating that dinner with someone special.

Bottom line, deferred gratification helps you put things in perspective while giving you time to think through your purchases. As a result, you'll have more money for passive income-generating investments and you'll really appreciate something when you buy or do it. Yahoo!

You don't need to be a rocket scientist to be successful!

When I was young, I thought you had to be really really smart to be successful. A rocket scientist. But that's not true!

To become financially successful:

1. Live below your means;

2. Bank your money;

3. Buy passive income-producing assets.

These three simple steps will bring you financial success, guaranteed. Just KISS it: Keep it Simple Sam.

If you have **credit card debt, don't** go on vacation!

Some people live with credit card debt. Some people think, well, this is just the way it is, my life seems to be fine. But your life is not fine. If you have credit card debt, you are wasting your money paying high interest AND you are living beyond your means.

Cut your expenses and pay it off. Credit card debt is really expensive and it is dumber than dumb. Paying all that interest to the bank and mortgaging your future. Choose to live below your means, save your money, and get rid of that debt! If your friends live with credit card debt you may think it is normal, but it is only normal for losers. Be a winner. Be free of credit card debt!

Saving money
doesn't mean
you won't have a fabulous day.

Savoring life is what it's all about. It is the Zen of living. Saving your money and deferring gratification doesn't mean you won't live a double-fabulous life. You can enjoy every little piece of your world today. All you need to do is realize that you don't have to spend all of your money to do it!

Have a picnic. Take a sunset walk with your sweetie. Splurge on some artisan fudge. The world is full of wonderful experiences that are free or almost free. Seek these out and you'll find that money-free experiences can be some of the richest moments of your life!

Sometimes the harder path is the best path.
Work hard.

Borrowing money for college, going out with your pals at night, or buying a car upon graduation may be easy, but it's probably not the best path. Taking the first job offer for a position you really don't love probably is not the best decision.

A good example of a great path that is a little more difficult is to have a part-time job while you are in school (high school and college). Do that, and with a little help from your parents, you may not need to borrow for college. How great not to be up to your knees in debt when you graduate from college! Also, when you are busy with studying and a part-time job, you learn to work hard and to budget your time. And employers rank potential employees higher if they worked their way through school!

It's important to work really hard to find a job you love. To work really hard to find a bargain in your living accommodations. To work really hard to keep your expenses low. Then bank your money and create passive income. Understand that choosing the path is as important as walking on the path you choose.

Having a million bucks
is better
than looking like a million bucks.

The main challenge for most people who are trying to create passive income (and passive income is the goal) is to live below their means. Living below your means is the practice of spending less money than you earn. It's so important to live below your means because you will never be able to invest in assets that create passive income if you can't save money. And you can't save money unless you live below your means. It's that simple.

So instead of looking like a million bucks (fancy clothes and car), put your money away and have a million bucks. Don't buy the big house and the fancy car. The expensive clothes and the newest gadget. Don't worry about looking like a million bucks. Instead, have a million bucks.

Visualize your savings.

Use a spreadsheet to visualize what it takes to live on less money and to see what a big impact cutting expenses can make on your bottom line. A spreadsheet helps you (and your sweetheart) understand what your financial habits (and habits generally) cost you. Do the work and create the spreadsheet!

If you don't buy the $4 daily latte and put the money in the bank instead, after ten years you'll have saved $19,665 (at 6% interest). After twenty years, you'll have saved $55,442. Would you rather have a latte or a rental house? Take the time to build a spreadsheet and really look at how *small changes lead to big gains.* And then visualize what you'll do with those gains. What kind of rental house? What kind of passive investment? What kind of future do you want?

A dollar not spent is a dollar you can save.

It's true! A dollar not spent is a dollar you can save. So take a close look at your expenses and figure out which expenses you can cut immediately. I know you can immediately:

1. Reduce your cell plan, and get rid of a landline if you have one;
2. Reduce your TV expenses (Comcast, Hulu, Netflix etc.);
3. Get a better deal on your car/life/homeowners' insurance;
4. Do your own landscaping. Always cut your own grass;
5. Wash your own car;
6. Buy clothes at Costco or a thrift store (I did it while making well over six figures!);
7. Use a crockpot to conveniently make large portions for less money;
8. Eat lower on the food chain. Beans and rice are great and cheap;
9. Prepared food and most meats are expensive, so prepare the food yourself and avoid expensive meat;
10. Meal plan so you have less food waste;
11. Cook from scratch and avoid expensive processed food. It's more healthy and will cost you less;
12. Buy beverages half as often;
13. Eat out half as often.

With a little effort you can immediately reduce your expenses and start putting those savings in the bank. And remember, putting money in the bank is the first step towards generating passive income. And passive income is the goal!

You don't need a new car; you want a new car.

Almost everyone needs to buy a car at some point in their lives. And the ads tell us we really need to buy a new car. So, when most folks think about buying a car, they are thinking about buying a new car. Sometimes a really fancy new car. But that's a terrible idea! Your ego might like a new car, but you really don't need a new car. *You just want a new car.*

Until 2018, I was driving the oldest car out of all my employees. I was driving the oldest car out of all my friends. It was a fabulous twelve-year old Camry. I loved that car. It never broke. It just drove. And best of all, my ego was not associated with my car. It was just a car, with no car payment.

Be smart with your money and buy a used car. What's the difference between buying a new car with $10,000 down and $40,000 financed versus buying a $10,000 used car and saving your money? *It ends up being a $100,000 swing!* Take that dough and invest it in income-producing assets. You'll be both smarter and richer!

Work and save while you're young
vs.
play and spend your passive income when you're old.

It's a pretty interesting contrast. If you save your money while you're younger, you'll be creating passive income when you're older. And your smart choices will allow you to rely on that income to play as you get older. *If you choose to play rather than save when you're younger, you'll still be working when you're older*, while the people who saved their money and created passive income will be playing. The choice is yours. But do you really want to be working when you're 70? Plan accordingly!

How the **rich** get **rich!**

The rich got rich and the rich get richer the same way you can get rich. It all starts with their thoughts and actions, that is - **your thoughts and actions!** The rich think over the long-term, not the short-term. The rich think about long-term gratification rather than short-term satisfaction. Their thoughts and actions in the past are responsible for the life they live today.

So start thinking like a rich person. Create Championship Habits while you are a beginner! Increase your savings, decrease your burn. Visualize how you will invest the savings, and how those savings will bring you financial success. Imagine sitting on the beach while your investments are generating the cash to pay for the pineapple juice in your hand. Visualization is such a powerful tool to achieve financial success. Be rich my friend. There is no downside!

I don't have any extra money to save.
Wrong!

If necessary, start by saving $1.00 per week (it is a start AND it will create a habit). Anyone can find one extra dollar per week to save. If you don't have a savings account, open one. In fact, I suggest you open a new savings account anyway - even if you already have one - where you can stash your $1.00 per week (or $10.00 or $100.00 or $1,000.00). A new account for a new you.

When you realize you can save a dollar a week, start looking at all of your expenses and figure out how to reduce those expenses. Make it a game. See how many of your expenses you can cut: fixed expenses like cell phones and TV, and discretionary expenses like lattes and eating out. Then think about how to reduce long-term expenses like your living and transportation choices. Can you take public transit? Rent out that extra room?

With a little effort, you can take that $1.00 in savings and easily make it many hundreds or thousands. Play the game. Enjoy the game. And watch your savings grow!

Live simply.

Living more simply has an intrinsic benefit and it just feels good. Can you take the bus to work? Do you need a landline in your home? Do you really need a new car or a car payment What can you do to live more simply and spend less money?

Living simply allows you freedom - mental freedom and economic freedom - as you grow your passive income! For many years I lived in a lovely basement apartment paying $1,000 per month. I had a shared hot tub, and a garage for my car. It was quite nice. My son called me a "minimalist," which I appreciated! So choose to live simply, grow your wealth, and enjoy the freedom that comes with making good choices!

What can I do to spend less money?

When you spend less money, you have more money to save and create passive income. It takes a little bit of thought, a little bit of discipline, and a little bit of action to spend less money. ***Being frugal is simply a mindset.*** But a desire to be successful is the key.

How about making coffee at home instead of going out for a $5 coffee? How about saving $10 to $15 a day by making your own lunch? That really adds up. How about washing your own car - every time you go through the carwash it's $10 to $15. Just by making these three changes, you can save $100 per week! Be smarter than the average bear - spend less and save big!

Stretch to buy income-producing property,
not a bigger house.

Stretching financially to buy a bigger house gets you nowhere. Stretching financially to buy a rental property, duplex, four-plex, or ten-plex is brilliant. If you focus on stuff: fancy cars, fancy houses, and fancy vacations, then you'll end up with worthless possessions, a bunch of liabilities. Stretch (for the right thing) and be somebody!

When you read *Rich Dad Poor Dad* you find out that revenue-generating real estate is an asset and your house is a liability. Stretch to buy income-producing assets, particularly real estate. But don't stretch to buy a bigger house. When you stretch like that, what you pull may be the rip-cord on your golden years.

Your small choices today will make a big difference tomorrow!

Today, instead of buying that new fishing boat, put the money in the bank. That money in the bank grows, allowing you to buy a rental house. Down the road that rental house will pay for your kids' education, it will supplement your retirement, and it can help pay for lots of great trips and fishing boats!

Today, instead of dessert, go for a walk with your sweetheart. Making your lunch every day for a month seems small, but over time it becomes huge. You will be saving money and eating healthier! Think about it - small decisions today have great effects tomorrow. Make good small choices today and you'll have the option later on to make good big choices. Choose to live smart one choice at a time!

That fancy new car will soon be an old used car.

Your beautiful new car. Shiny. You feel like a million bucks driving that car home. Beautiful. The wheels are so cool. You are ten feet tall. But the reality is the value dropped a ton driving off the lot, and the value goes down every single day. Pretty soon, after six months or a year, you're not going to keep it quite as clean as you did when you first got it. And the value is still going down, down, down. And then it's just an old used car.

When you drive down the street and look at a beautiful new Lexus or Tesla, remind yourself that in five years it will just be an old used car. So put your money to work in something positive, something long term that **GROWS** in value. Buy something that's going to appreciate and pay you (that is the definition of passive income). A new car, a beautiful new car, is simply a transient pleasure. Instead, buy the gift that keeps on giving: income-producing real estate, stocks, or bonds. But not a car my friend.

Cut your own grass.

I have a friend who has a lawn service cut his grass. This is not necessarily a bad thing, but it is a waste of money. My friend is not a millionaire. He does not have any passive income. The rule of thumb should be: ***cut your own grass until you are a millionaire***. If you need a mower, buy one from a yard sale or Craigslist. Why waste your money on a new mower?! Pretty simple, and it's just another way to reduce your expenses and free up money for passive income. Make sense? Use a push-mower and get a workout in while you do it!

Live below your means
so when Mr. Opportunity knocks
you will be able to answer!

Opportunities are all over the place. They're not available every day, but they are available every other day. Save your money and have some cash available so when Mr. Opportunity knocks, you will be able to answer.

The stock market takes a tumble and you'll be able to invest. The real estate market slows down and you'll be able to buy a nice rental property. The older you get, the more friends and business associates you have and that will result in learning about more opportunities. Put yourself in a winner's position by having money available to invest when Mr. Opportunity comes along.

Become a Super Saver!

Once you learn how to save on a consistent basis, you can classify yourself as a saver! This is a great label because it denotes that you're taking pride in being a saver, that saving is important to you. The next step is to become a Super Saver and accelerate your path to independence. Accelerate your path to passive income. Accelerate your path to freedom. Becoming a Super Saver means putting a larger percentage of your take-home pay in the bank, in your savings. One of the best ways to do this is to reduce your expenses. Another critical element is to have at least 10% of your take home pay automatically put in a savings account (a never touch, passive income only account). Get a roommate to help cover your rent or mortgage payment. Drive a used car. Don't go out as much. Figure it out. Be smart. Become a Super Saver!

MIF: Money is freedom.

This is really simple. Money gives you the freedom to do what you want.

Money doesn't have anything to do with greed or avarice, or not being interested in people, or not being holistic. In fact, money allows you to be holistic, to be interested in people, to take care of your family, to travel, to support causes that you think are important.

Money gives you the freedom to do what you want. And the most freedom comes from passive income - that way your money is working for you rather than you working for your money. Let your money give you the freedom to buy organic food, to travel when you want, to take care of your family. **Money is freedom,** and that's just wonderful.

You don't have to buy new stuff.

Most people think that when they buy clothes or furniture or household supplies that they need to buy new stuff. Some people believe that they need to buy not just new stuff, but the expensive stuff. These folks think that used clothing or furniture is for poor people or for people without a steady income. But that's just not true!

With the goal of living below your means, with the goal of creating passive income, with the goal of saving money and putting money in the bank, buy used stuff! Go to Goodwill and buy some clothes or furniture. There are great deals and great things at Goodwill! Get on the internet. Get on Craigslist. Find yard sales and garage sales. Go to consignment shops.

Again, make it a game. A treasure hunt. And the treasure is savings! Because every dollar you save is a dollar you can put in the bank. And every dollar in the bank is one dollar closer to passive income, or more passive income. And passive income is a heck of a lot more comfortable than a new sofa.

The deals you don't do
are more important
than the deals you do.

If you make a big mistake with an investment, you can lose your total investment. Up front, try to figure out what big mistakes are staring you in the face: is the freeway going in on the other side of town; could this building have mold; could this person you're dealing with be a criminal, not trustworthy, or dishonest?

Big mistakes are only one decision away, so always be ready to walk. **Because the deals you don't do are more important than the deals you do.** Sometimes it is easier to lose money than to make money. Take your time, analyze the investment, and figure out how to minimize your chances of making a big mistake. Don't get too greedy. Greed is the enemy of success, and so is impatience. And always be ready to say no.

Take your time finding deals and don't try to make all the money at one time. To mitigate the mistakes you're bound to make, remember to spread your investments around. Don't put all your eggs in one basket. Even if a deal looks fabulous, do not put all your money in one deal! Take this to heart, and you'll be on your way to investing in winners and building a portfolio!

Create an annual financial statement.

Everyone should do an annual financial statement. A financial statement gives you a snapshot of your financial world all in one place. And after you've done it for a few years, you can track your progress. And by progress, I mean creating and growing your passive income. Progress means having your money work for you rather than you working for your money. You can set up the financial statement in Excel so it is easy to do and easy to access. There are also plenty of companies online offering similar financial dashboards.

I know that creating an annual financial statement is one of the main drivers for understanding financial literacy and creating passive income. It is important to involve your sweetheart in this activity so you both are on the same page and moving in the same direction. So set some goals, track your progress, and watch that money grow!

Save for a rainy day.

You need to save your money for a rainy day. You never know when something will break. You never know when your roof will start leaking. You never know when the furnace will go out. So create a savings account for a rainy day (an account that is separate from your passive income fund). When the skies open up, you'll have cash to take care of the problem, rather than going into debt to fix the issue. So be smart. Save for a rainy day.

Wash your own car!

Same friend, same story. My friend runs his car through the car wash at $10 to $15 a pop. But that's $10 or $15 per week that could go in the bank. Don't waste your money. Be aware of your expenses. My friend says he washes his car because it's better for the environment. I think this is baloney. My friend just never developed the skill of reducing his burn (spending less money), being careful with expenses, and creating passive income. Are you ready to develop more skills today? Take action (Kicksumass Today!) and wash your own car!

Don't go into debt to pay for college
(or at least minimize borrowing).

Graduating from college with a lot of debt makes it harder to save your money and create passive income. A bunch of debt will take decades to pay off. To avoid getting out of college with a lot of debt, work while you're going to college. To avoid getting out of college with a lot of debt, live really cheaply while you're going to college. Consider living at home and going to community college for the first two years. Eat in more. Don't go out with your friends as much. Work during college. Work experience will put you far ahead in the job market. Work experience will also make you tougher and smarter and stronger! Make smart choices and think about your bottom line.

The key to saving when you get out of college is simply to minimize your borrowing during college, and work to make up the rest. If you have no student loan debt (or at least not very much), then the money that was going to go to debt payments can now go in your savings account instead. Bottom line: getting out of college with a lot of debt and no work experience is for losers. But you're a winner, so work hard, study hard. But go easy on the borrowing.

Meet Steve. He's my hero.

Steve is a friend of mine and he's my hero. Steve is my hero because by the time he was 29 and purchased his first home (as his personal residence) he already had five rental houses. Steve is just an average guy. School was hard for him so he decided to work really hard at it. What a concept! And he never stopped working hard.

Steve epitomizes deferred gratification and living below your means. What a smart guy. By doing this he wasn't living like a monk or having a terrible time. He was young, having fun and working on his rental properties. Building passive income. Now in his early 50s, most people would say he's wealthy. Steve appreciates the value of a dollar. He appreciates the value of hard work. He is a living testament that building passive income early is the bomb. So be like Steve and get on it early! And you can be my hero too!

Bring your lunch
to work
until your car is paid off!

If you have a car payment, don't eat out! Having a car payment and paying interest to the bank is not a good use of your money, so you want to get out from under that payment as quickly as possible. Save money elsewhere and put the savings toward the car loan. For example, if you eat out every workday, you are spending at least $300 per month. Using those savings to pay down the car loan will get it paid off double-quick. Now imagine where else you can save money and get that car paid off in one year. Get the point?! A side note is that if you bring a smoothie for lunch, as I do, you will be healthier AND pay off the car quickly!

What gets more valuable over time: a boat, a plane, or a rental house?

Few things get more valuable over time. A boat goes down in value fast. A plane, even faster. But over time, real estate goes up in value. That is, real estate appreciates. Not always, but almost always. Because real estate is slow and steady. Real estate is for the long game. The daily choices we make affect our future, so spend thoughtfully.

Put the odds of an asset appreciating on your side. Buy real estate and hold it. In fact, if you want to increase your odds of success then buy a "fixer" to work on and improve (and raise the rent) AND you will make more money and reduce your risk! Then, buy more real estate. Pretty soon, your smart choices will fatten your bank account. And you can use all that wonderful passive income to enjoy a very comfortable lifestyle and all the good stuff that comes with it. Yahoo!

Cash flow
v.
assets.

There are some people who have great cash flow and think they're rich because they have a bunch of money coming in allowing them to buy boats, cars, motor homes, renovations, furniture, and travel.

Well, when somebody has great cash flow but no passive income-generating assets they are just dumb. Unlike all that work to get the cash flow, real assets actually make money while you sleep. Assets are revenue-generating, and the goal is to own revenue generating assets. Don't waste great cash flow. Don't be that person who is working his tail off creating a lot of income and who then just blows it on junk. You don't want to be 65 and still working your tail off!

And what about retirement, or slowing down? Without smart choices during the big cash flow days, there won't be any way to slow down because you have to keep the revenue up to pay for all the stuff! So be smart. Don't buy stuff. Invest. And put that fabulous cash flow to work. We want our money to work for us rather than us working for our money!

<u>NOTES</u>

Pillar III – Health

Pay attention to what you eat, listen to your body, and get ready for a long and healthy life.

Health Section Overview:

Health is just so important. You can have all the time and money in the world, but if you have poor health, there's no real way to truly enjoy it. The information in this section is critical if you want to live long and be healthy (think about it as a healthspan rather than a lifespan), and enjoy the wealth you create along the way. The health section stresses personal responsibility, because if you want to be healthy, well, it's up to you!

Personal responsibility dictates that you are responsible for your health. You'll again find many hints, rules, and shortcuts about how to be healthier. It still amazes me that most people don't really pay attention to what they put in their mouth and that what they put in their mouth makes all the difference to their health. There is a direct connection between your health and what you eat. Being healthy starts with a choice, the choice of wanting to be healthy.

If you want to be healthy, you only need to look at your actions. If you're not eating well, not eating raw and fresh, then you must alter your behavior. The first step is knowledge, but the next step is action. Be a person of action and move towards health!

Eat *low-calorie high-nutrient* foods like fresh fruits and vegetables.

One of the big rules for a great diet and a healthy body is to eat *low-calorie high-nutrient food*. What fits that definition? Raw fruits and vegetables. The more raw fruits and vegetables you eat, the healthier you will be. Think of low-calorie high-nutrient food as the standard.

Sometimes what happens is you go on the program, eating fresh fruits and vegetables. Fresh and raw fruits and vegetables. I'm on it. I'm excited. But then you fall off the wagon and go and have beer and pizza one night. That is not evil. That's just human. I love pizza. It's not a problem to have a pizza every once in a while. But get back to the fruits and veggies afterwards. The more organic fresh fruits and vegetables you eat, the better off you'll be. The more organic raw fruits and vegetables you eat, the healthier you will be. Less disease and a longer life. Yahoo!

Age more slowly.
Eat real, fresh wonderful food.

To reduce cellular decay and help you age more slowly, eat fresh organic unprocessed fruits and vegetables. Processed foods like most meats, hamburgers, white bread, snack food, fried potatoes, and puffed cheesy corn are all garbage that just wear you out. Processed food is harder for your body to digest and it is not healthy to eat!

Fresh organic greens are way easier on your system. So eat real food and you'll be happier, healthier, live longer, your skin will be brighter and your eyes clearer, and your memory will improve. How good is that!

And think about this: as I look at my friends who are my age (70 as I'm writing this), those who have aged the fastest almost universally eat garbage (alcohol, fast food, snacks). Note that it's a continuum. It's not like a slice of pizza will kill you. But if you eat pizza every day, you'll age faster. To age well, eat real, fresh wonderful food. Your mind and body will thank you!

Drink clean water!

When you drink water out of a plastic bottle (the kind you buy at the store that crinkles) the plastic is leached into the water, so you're drinking some plastic with your water. Yuk!

When I bring water to work or when I carry water with me, I do it in a clean glass bottle. Buy a couple of glass bottles with rubber protection around them, or stainless-steel water bottles, and take one wherever you go. They're terrific and you get clean water.

At home we distill our water. I want to get all the glyphosate and chlorine and fluoride out of the water that I'm drinking. A distiller sits on the counter and gives us clean water! And remember to put a pinch of sea salt into the distilled water for added minerals. Most water systems have fluoride and chlorine added to it - that stuff is poison that you do not want to ingest. So carry filtered, clean water with you. You'll thank yourself! You will also be creating more healthy habits!

Make one meal each day raw and fresh!

Make sure one of your meals each and every day is raw and fresh. The best way to do this is with a Vitamix smoothie! I often have a smoothie for lunch and a salad for dinner. These are fresh and raw meals. And they don't add any weight to the scale of poor health and disease. Eat raw and fresh and you will be happy that you did.

Another reason to eat raw and fresh is for the lovely olive oil you can put on the salad. My salad dressing is only olive oil and balsamic vinegar. Try to purchase high quality olive oil, which tastes better and is really healthy for you. Be a winner my friend and get fresh.

More is *not* better!

Whether it's a meal out or a batch of chocolate chip cookies, more is not better. My sweetheart and I just split a chocolate chip cookie and it was fabulous. These are fancy gourmet chocolate chip cookies and a whole cookie would have just been too much. Splitting the cookie was wonderful. And less cookie is more health!

One more glass of wine isn't going to make you any cooler. Having two cookies isn't any better than half a cookie. Often when we go out to dinner, we will split an entree. More entree is not better. Less calories equals less fat around my tummy, and more paper on the health and longevity side of the scale.

Also, really appreciating what you are eating is a lovely way to have a Zen attitude about life. Being grateful and appreciative are lovely perspectives you can choose. But when it comes to things we put in our bodies, more is generally not better!

Health 101.

Time to *change things up*. One of the first steps you can take to become healthier is to change things up. Let's start with 30 days from the moment you read this. Eliminate carbs from your diet. No bread, no pasta, no crackers, no cookies. No processed wheat of any kind. So nothing in the snack aisle. In fact, there isn't much you can eat down the grocery store aisles. It is way better to shop the edges of the store to get rid of those simple, brutal carbs that we all love. I promise you, when you eliminate those carbs you will feel better. You will lose weight. And with that, all sorts of good things will come to you! The idea of changing things up is a wonderful concept that applies to every area of our lives! Go change things up!

Eating carbs is just like eating sugar.

Most carbs turn into sugar right after you eat them. So eating carbs is just like eating sugar. And sugar stresses your system. Sugar causes your body to pump out insulin. Sugar causes your body to be under a bit of stress and to pump out a bit of cortisol. And cortisol ages you. Not good!

So if you want to lose weight, if you want to be healthier, if you want to have nicer skin, it's simple: eat more fresh organic fruits and vegetables. And stay away from the carbs. A wonderful tip is to clean the carbs out of your kitchen (throw them out) and you will be less likely to eat those bad little carbs! Simple as that. Easy peasy.

I just had a physical and my doctor says I'm fine.

Great! Kind of.....The problem is your doctor does not know how to weigh all of the pieces of paper you put on the scale of death and disease. She can measure your cholesterol, take your pulse, and look for high blood pressure, but your doctor cannot and does not understand all of the pieces of paper on the scale, all of the negative events that you've piled on the scale. The best thing you can do is look forward proactively. *Slow the aging process down by eating real food.* Things like organic fruits and vegetables. Nuts and beans. They taste great and are wonderful for you. Help your doctor out. Put less weight on the scale of death and disease, and more weight on mindful and healthy living. ***Take personal responsibility (PR) for your health.*** Just because your doctor says you are doing well does not really mean you can continue the way you are going. Remember, most doctors treat symptoms, not the root causes of disease. So it's up to you my friend. Yahoo - take responsibility for your health!

Health 102.

More change. Next step: ***get off meat for a month***. No meat, so no bacon, no hamburgers, no chicken or steak. No fish. Sounds terrible, right? Wrong! Give it a shot for a month. You'll be amazed at how good you look and feel AND the ability to change things up will make you a more powerful person!

I know it sounds hard, maybe. Maybe just change things up for one week! Do it one day at a time. The whole purpose is to let you know that you're in charge of your health and your life. Also, to see how you feel after a month of no meat. You won't regret it. Change things up and be a winner, Yahoo!

Health in a Vitamix!

Believe it or not, drinking a meal from your Vitamix draws a straight line to health. When you use a Vitamix, you're blending together all these raw and fresh organic vegetables and fruits. I put more vegetables (greens!) in my drinks and less fruit. You just gotta love fresh, organic raw greens. Drinking a smoothie like this will keep you younger. Your system won't be stressed from processed food. You won't have the poison from animal meat. Generally, I drink a Vitamix smoothie five days a week for lunch. It is easy, tastes good, and is wonderful for my body (and easy to digest).

Also, when you drink a Vitamix smoothie, the fruits and vegetables are way more digestible than eating the same fruits and vegetables in their natural form - the ratio is something like 9 times more bioavailability to your body when you blend versus simply eating the ingredients. I like those kinds of numbers and such information encourages me to enjoy a smoothie every day! Give it a try. One Vitamix meal a day for 30 days. I promise that you'll see and feel the difference!

Mistake #1 of unhealthy people: They eat garbage food!

I was recently waiting to get on an airplane and there were a couple of folks near the gate who were younger than me, sitting in wheelchairs and eating processed fried chicken parts. Isn't it obvious when you eat garbage the results will not be good? These people have probably been eating processed food for the past fifty years, and they looked like it. Obese, poor skin, and wheelchair-bound. Don't be like that.

Instead, stay young. ***Eat low-calorie high-nutrition food.*** It's really not very complicated. But every bite you take makes a difference. Every choice is a piece of paper on the scale of death and disease or health and longevity.

Choose health when you're younger because your body can take lots of abuse and not show it. As you age, the weight of those unhealthy decisions will drag you towards disease. If you choose health, you will simply stay younger longer! Choose health my friends!

What to do when you get a cold.

Many of us can feel a cold coming on. Sometimes your eyes are sensitive when you look left and right. Sometimes you're a little stuffed up or sneezy. Sometimes you feel fatigued.

When you feel a cold coming on, double up on clean water. Double up on the vitamin C. A good choice is liposomal vitamin C. Liposomal vitamin C helps increase the amount of vitamin C your body can absorb, which can be a wonderful defense against colds. Grab a Neti pot and pour some salted water through your sinuses. I also gargle with salt water when I have a sore throat or feel a cold coming on. Gargling kills those bacteria - and it doesn't let them grow well, so gargling can also be a great deterrent to a cold. Get to bed early and have a nice sleep. Sleep is a big healer. And at the first sign of a cold, I spray some colloidal silver up my nose! I also enjoy Braggs apple cider vinegar, it has a tart taste but it also helps you stay healthy! Stay well my friends!

Start every day
with two **big** glasses of water.

Water does lots of good stuff for you. Water helps you stay healthy. Water moves good and bad stuff through your system. Did you know if you're hydrated it's way tougher to catch a cold? And if you're hydrated, it's way easier to think clearly. **There is literally no downside to drinking water.** Start your day on a positive note - drink two big glasses of water. You'll feel the difference, and you'll be building a healthy habit that will improve your life! *Creating good habits becomes a habit!*

Health 103, the combo!

Now you've learned how good you feel when you're off carbs for a month. You also know how good you feel when you're off meat for a month. Now do the combo, the ultimate health month. **Stay off carbs and meat for a month.** Out with the garbage, in with the beautiful fruits and vegetable, beans and legumes. You will feel fabulous and start to look fabulous! All these healthy changes will change your life! How powerful is that!

The food you keep in your kitchen makes a huge difference to your health!

The food in your kitchen - the cookies, the peanuts, the little snacks, basically the high-carb food in your pantry, makes a huge difference in your health and your weight. I am a snacker. When I get home, I enjoy a little snack. Same before bed. What I have done is get the unhealthy snacks out of my house. Sorry, no cookies, crackers, or even bread in my house. I think about all the cheese toast I have eaten in past. Wow! If it is not in the house, you can't eat it!

Do a little inventory and look at the snacks in your cupboard. If you have those little packs of high-carb snacks, throw them out. Carbs are just terrible. Waffle mix? Very yummy, but if you have a waffle maker on your counter and you're 40 pounds overweight, the waffle maker should be in the basement. Take a look at what's in the pantry and get rid of the all the garbage carbs. Your mind and body will thank you.

You do not catch cancer.

Having systemic cancer is often the result of poor lifestyle choices. That is, cancer is often the result of your behavior. And carbs can assist cancer. Carbs turn into sugar and cancer cells feed on sugar. We all have cancer cells in our body (erratic cellular reproduction), but the more sugar we give the cancer cells the worse it gets.

You don't catch cancer - *your behavior and lifestyle lead to cancer.* What are the positive behaviors you can do to avoid cancer? What are the negative behaviors you can cut out to improve your health? The first thing to do is eat organic food and avoid carbs. **Eat mainly a *plant-based diet.*** It's fresh and nutritious, and it's not feeding the cancer. If you are a big smoker or drinker, cut that stuff way back, or stop. Eat better, drink less, and you're on your way!

Carbs equal sugar.

When you eat most carbs - things like rice, bread, and pasta - the carbs very quickly turn into sugar in your system. If you want to gain weight, if you want to be heavy, if you want to be sick, eat more carbs. And cancer loves sugar, so if you like cancer, eat more carbs. I am not trying to be a smart ass, but it is so true: carbs really hurt your chances of being healthy!

If you want to be healthy, if you want to live a long time and not have a gut, eat less carbs. The question is what do you eat instead of carbs? The answer is more organic raw fruits and vegetables. Salads are wonderful. I always eat one meal a day of raw fruits and vegetables, usually two. Generally, in the morning I have some fresh fruit. For lunch or dinner, I'll have a big salad or a smoothie. Look at the Vitamix chapter. It'll tell you what to do, which is to eat high-nutrition, low-calorie foods. Just what we're looking for!

Beware of the words "Enriched White Flour" on any food label.

Enriched White Flour means that all the nutrients (about twenty of them) are stripped (by mechanical or chemical means) out of the flour, and then a few synthetic vitamins (about five) are thrown back into the flour. The stripped-out items also include the fiber (bran and wheat germ) and phytonutrients. This label sounds healthy and good but it is just the opposite!

So Enriched White Flour on the label means "do not eat," because it is essentially sugar plus a poor multi-vitamin. When you're looking at any white bread products (sandwich bread, buns, tortillas) avoid any of those products that say Enriched White Flour on the label because it's nothing but cell-destroying garbage.

Health is habits.

As you hit your thirties and forties you will find that you come to a metaphysical fork in the road. What happens is if you are unhealthy, overweight, eat too much junk, and don't exercise then you will be taking the path more traveled and your health will gradually go down the tube. Choose the healthy path. ***Understand that your health is simply good habits*** - high-nutrition low-calorie food, lots of water, exercise, and a positive mental attitude. Meditate. Do it all. Be healthy and go for it!

Show me a big drinker and I'll show you a loser.

If you drink a lot, if you drink every night, you're going to be a loser. You can never do any critical thinking after one or two beverages. Generally, after a couple of drinks, all you are good for is watching TV. You cannot really relate to another human if you have had a couple of drinks.

To be successful, you must do deep, critical thinking. Reading a book is active and it generally cannot happen after a couple of drinks. And that kind of critical thinking is absolutely necessary if you're going to better yourself (health, wealth, and mindset). When you're thinking deeply, you'll read more books. You'll work on your relationships. You'll save your money. Being successful happens little by little. And a lot of drinking won't help. Make the choice and choose health!

Never eat fast food!!

I could go on and on but it's a very simple rule. ***Never eat fast food***. Or a positive way to say the same thing: only eat healthful food. There is so much garbage in fast food that you just want to avoid. Highly processed, hormone and drug loaded, poisonous animal fat. Highly processed flour. Sweet soft drinks with high fructose corn syrup. All terrible for you.

Make your own lunch if necessary (in fact if you make your own lunch, as I do, you will probably have a healthier lunch AND save money!). Start reading about health. Smarter people are healthier. Not IQ smarts - book smarts. You don't have to be born with a high IQ to read a good book. So, read about health. Make health your hobby. The more you read, the more you realize that you should never eat fast food. Become an elitist, a health elitist!

One piece of paper doesn't weigh very much.

One piece of paper on the scale of death and disease - meaning one event: a cheeseburger and fries or a deep-dish pizza or a big steak or excessive drinking - is not very much. But over time these very small, seemingly insignificant events add up. Pretend that each unhealthy event is one piece of paper on the scale of death and disease. And pretty soon you will have 100, 500, 5,000, or 10,000 pieces of paper on the disease side of the scale. Look at your friends who live big or hard, who are big drinkers, big fast-food eaters. They get sick younger. They die younger. So next time you have the choice, don't put the paper on the wrong side of the scale. Choose health and longevity, not death and disease. What a concept. YOU get to choose your path!

So what's wrong with a burger and fries?

Wow! Let me count the ways a hamburger and fries are terrible for you. The bun on the hamburger is an ultra-processed food-like substance that turns into sugar immediately upon ingestion (blood sugar spike!) and provides zero nutritional value. Perhaps worse, that kind of mass-produced wheat product probably contains glysophate because the wheat fields were sprayed with this cancer-causing chemical to keep the weeds down. **Yikes!**

For the meat, your typical ground beef is made from parts of the cow that can't be processed into any other edible product. The "meat" is often held together with some type of chemical bonding agent. And none of this mentions the high dose of antibiotics that can be found in most ground beef. It's just terrible. Put down the burger and fries and pick up something that actually nourishes you. After thirty days of no burgers and fries, I promise you that you'll feel the difference.

<u>NOTES</u>

Closing Thoughts

I sincerely hope that this book, or just one of the thoughts in this book, changes your life. *A Viking's Guide to Wealth and Health* is not something to read once and put on a bookshelf. This book is designed to be opened regularly to any page, where your intuition will guide you to some thought that will inspire you. Life is all about inspiration, so go be inspired because it is truly up to you!

ABOUT THE AUTHOR

The author splits his time between a South American rainforest where he helps local people plant ornamental flowers and Nepal where he helps the Nepalese with their yak grooming. Just kidding. John Bredvik lives in Seattle with his sweetheart Jan.

NOTES